ONCE UPON A DREAM

Poems From Kent

Edited By Jenni Harrison

First published in Great Britain in 2019 by:

Young Writers
Remus House
Coltsfoot Drive
Peterborough
PE2 9BF
Telephone: 01733 890066
Website: www.youngwriters.co.uk

All Rights Reserved
Book Design by Ashley Janson
© Copyright Contributors 2019
Softback ISBN 978-1-78988-844-7
Hardback ISBN 978-1-83928-250-8
Printed and bound in the UK by BookPrintingUK
Website: www.bookprintinguk.com
YB0417P

FOREWORD

Welcome Reader, to a world of dreams.

For Young Writers' latest competition, we asked our writers to dig deep into their imagination and create a poem that paints a picture of what they dream of, whether it's a make-believe world full of wonder or their aspirations for the future.

The result is this collection of fantastic poetic verse that covers a whole host of different topics. Let your mind fly away with the fairies to explore the sweet joy of candy lands, join in with a game of fantasy football, or you may even catch a glimpse of a unicorn or another mythical creature. Beware though, because even dreamland has dark corners, so you may turn a page and walk into a nightmare!

Whereas the majority of our writers chose to stick to a free verse style, others gave themselves the challenge of other techniques such as acrostics and rhyming couplets. We also gave the writers the option to compose their ideas in a story, so watch out for those narrative pieces too!

Each piece in this collection shows the writers' dedication and imagination – we truly believe that seeing their work in print gives them a well-deserved boost of pride, and inspires them to keep writing, so we hope to see more of their work in the future!

CONTENTS

Marlborough Centre, Hoo

Aymen Amoura (11)	1
Logan Barkel (9)	2
Leon Kwapong (11)	3
Chloe Hurran (10)	4
Ena Alina Osaji (11)	5
Jack Dale (11)	6

Milstead & Frinsted CE Primary School, Milstead

Morgane Argivier (11)	7
Isabel Lee (11)	8
Jessica Robyn Cracknell (11)	9

Newlands Primary School, Ramsgate

Kinslee Rickiel Henry (10)	10
Jamie Drew Blake (11)	12
Neil Cunningham (11)	13
Ryan Whitworth-Saker (11)	14
Esmae Franks (11)	15
Veja Razukeviciute (11)	16

Park Way Primary School, Maidstone

Kai Gardinor (11)	17
Ozge Ekinci (11)	18
Ivana Paynavelova (10)	20
Grace Bishop (10)	21
Bernards Brasas (11)	22
Alyssa Osborne (10)	23

Snodland CE Primary School, Snodland

Samuel Woolley (8)	24
Noah Taylor (9)	25
Chloe Theobald (7)	26
Laila Barton (8)	27
Charlotte Elizabeth Tricker (8)	28
Chelsea Rae Goodayle (8)	29
Ryley Daniel Chance (7)	30

St Katherine's School & Nursery, Snodland

AJ Ashton Volbrecht (11)	31
Dean Brewster (11)	32
Hope (11)	34
Harry Attwater (11)	36
Ethan Thomas Harewood (11)	38
Keira Rhiannon Montaner (11)	40
Thomas Benjamin Curley (11)	41
James Morris (11)	42
Bethany Kate Loveland (11)	43
Cooper Idle (10)	44
Elisha Pickup (10)	45
Sean Cardiff Keefe (10)	46
Shennai Hall (11)	47
Jake Gillett-Ward (11)	48
Alfie Thomas Moss (11)	49
Millie (11)	50
Isabella N (11)	51
Madison Wainwright (10)	52
Billy Moody (10)	53
Tilly-Marie Turgoose (11)	54
Grace (11)	55
Oscar Miles (11)	56

Olivia Nash Thompson (11)	57
Chloe (11)	58
Ciaran Oliver-Jones (11)	59
Maria May Bowyer (11)	60
Brooke Amy Urbanowicz (11)	61
Daniel Stroud (11)	62
Ben Wade (11)	63
Taylor Mannerings (11)	64
Kyle Goodall (11)	65
Grace Wastell (11)	66
Chloe Annabelle Rosier (11)	67
Kai Hayes (10)	68
Cameron (11)	69
Sebastian Lane (10)	70
Louise Zoe Joan Waddell (11)	71
Rebecca Louise Daynes (11)	72
Izaac Sayers (11)	73
Evie-Mae Hawkins (11)	74
Skye-Olivia Harris (11)	75
Hollie Elizabeth Browne (10)	76
Mia Hamilton Greenstreet (10)	77

St Mark's CE Primary School, Tunbridge Wells

Rosie Jane Layberry (9)	78
Oliwia Zborowska (9)	79

St Martin's CE Primary School, Folkestone

Freya	80
Hayden John Bestford (11)	81
Katie Harris (11)	82
Jessica Wright (10)	83
Michael Guiver (11)	84
Alice Ellen Law (11)	86
Isabelle Lamb (11)	87
Seren-Mair Worrall (11)	88
Maya Briggs (10)	89
Evie Aitchison (11)	90
Izzy Taylor (11)	91
Hannah Hollows (10)	92
Jack Rolfe (10)	93

Morgan Baker-Goode (11)	94
Rohan Syred (11)	95
Hayley Conley (11)	96
Mollie Coughlan (11)	97
Jack Tumber (10)	98

St Peter & St Paul Catholic Primary Academy, St Paul's Wood Hill

Chimamanda Kaitlyn Afam (8)	99
Esen Arif (10)	100
Lucy Chisom Ekpe (10)	101
Isabelle Winkley (11)	102
Maria Barbashova (9)	103
Isabelle Keely Jones (11)	104

St Peter's CE Primary School, Folkestone

Joshua J (9) & Alfie M	105
Marika S (9) & Brandon	106
Emma Longley (8) & Emily-Rose Middleton	108
Olivia Sullivan (9), Kyle Horgan & Oscar J (8)	109
Jayden Michael J (8) & Sonny Haydn King	110
Ruby EC (8)	111
Amber J (9)	112
Leni Adelaide King (9)	113
Betsy P-B (8)	114
Tobias A D S Simpson (9)	115
Demi Leigh D (8)	116

St Teresa's Catholic Primary School, Ashford

Frankie Griffin-Greca (9)	117
Noah Brooks (8)	118
Sheena Ndduga (9)	120
Edward Badze (8)	121
Charlie Hall (8)	122
Nathan Deus Dedit Epulani (9)	123
Solomon Olajide (9)	124

Leon Jijo (9)	125
Molly Elizabeth James (8)	126
Ruben McQuillan (9)	127
Aldy Saffa (9)	128
Emilia Rebecca Skinner (9)	129
Gabriella Charlotte Pigram (9)	130
Isabel Johny (9)	131
Munashe Parsvell Mungoni (9)	132
Riley McQuillan (9)	133
Jessica Broome (9)	134

Sundridge & Brasted CE (VC) Primary School, Sundridge

Ruby Rae Mandry-Lowe (10)	135
Daisy Morgan (11)	136
Zachary Alex Harvey (11)	137
Tayla Rendle (10)	138
Chelsea Casserley (10)	139
Oscar Samways (11)	140
Jared Douglas Somerville (11)	141
Oscar Shadforth (10)	142
Harri Stubbings (11)	143

The Gateway Primary Academy, Dartford

Alana Heywood-Oriogun (9)	144
Clara Madalina Petcu (9)	146
Lily Barden (8)	147
Emilia Nathanael (8)	148
Neve McDonald Murray (8)	149
Sruthi Edara (8)	150
Isla McDonald Murray (8)	151
Benjamin Leachman (9)	152
Daniela Guwor (8)	153
Andrew Gruy (7)	154
Eva Odetah (7)	155
Scarlett Eve Leachman (7)	156
Jessica Hawney (8)	157
Lacey Underhill (7)	158

THE POEMS

Dinosaurs

D inosaurs lived in the Mesozoic, 100 million years ago on Earth
I n the past, reptiles went extinct millions of years ago
N on-dinosaurs on Earth include tyrannosaurus, stegosaurus
O n Earth this was a world ruled by dinosaurs
S tegosaurus lived in the Jurassic period, triceratops lived in the Cretaceous period
A llosaurs were carnivores
U p in the air, or in water, or on land, the small animal was a dinosaur
R eport of a meteor hit the Earth, dinosaurs became extinct
S nakes, lizards and humans all extinct animals, including stegosaurus, mammoth and smilodon.

Aymen Amoura (11)
Marlborough Centre, Hoo

Dreams

D ares in dreams
R eady for imagination
E xciting adventures
A mazing surprises
M aking things up
S ee you another day.

Logan Barkel (9)
Marlborough Centre, Hoo

Football

A t night I dream of Arsenal
R ed card
S hoot
E xcited
N ow a penalty
A mazing
L ondon team.

Leon Kwapong (11)
Marlborough Centre, Hoo

Unicorn

U nusual
N ice
I ce cream and chocolate
C aramel
O range
R unning slowly
N owhere.

Chloe Hurran (10)
Marlborough Centre, Hoo

Unicorn

U gly
N ice
I ce lolly
C old and sweet
O range
R ainbow burst
N ature.

Ena Alina Osaji (11)
Marlborough Centre, Hoo

Dinosaurs

Dinosaurs stomp
Dinosaurs chomp
They are lumpy and bumpy
They roar
And they all live together happily ever after.

Jack Dale (11)
Marlborough Centre, Hoo

I Had A Dream Last Night

I had a dream last night
Football fairies kick with all their might
Their numbers printed on their wings
The wild crowd roars and sings
Kicky ups, dribbling and the football flying
The ball goes in the goal diving

I had a dream last night
The grandma pirates are the centre of the fight
Cutlasses and swords, not at all
These pirates use needles and wool
Their mighty ship the Forty Winks
Is sailing away victorious from a close sink

I had a dream last night
The vampire teachers hate the light
For school dinners they'll eat raw meat
They'll bite if you're out of your seat
Or interrupt while they speak
The zombie headmaster you shall seek

Football fairies kick with all their might
The grandma pirates are the centre of the fight
The vampire teachers hate the light
Are all the dreams I had last night.

Morgane Argivier (11)
Milstead & Frinsted CE Primary School, Milstead

The Red-Haired Lady

It's the red-haired lady who's in my mind when I'm asleep
Her hair all neat in a bun when over my fence she does peep
I can't see her face due to the binoculars she uses
She makes me afraid as I don't know why it is me she chooses
From my bedroom window, I see a flash of red
Is it her I see as I get ready for bed?
I dream of her again, that she comes to the door
I feel so scared, I don't know if I can take it much more
I'm not sleeping well now, these dreams keeping me awake
I make my way to school, but my head really aches
In class we are told someone new starts today
Imagine my fear as in they walk
It's the red-haired lady
Now I know I'm definitely being stalked!

Isabel Lee (11)
Milstead & Frinsted CE Primary School, Milstead

The Theory Of Darkness

Darkness, no one knows
Exactly what to expect
Darkness, but is this a
Theory we should forget?

Darkness, is this a
Sight to be forgiven?
Darkness, it's like a
Car that should not be driven

Darkness, who knows
Where it will lead?
Darkness, it leaves
Traces of random deeds

Darkness...

Jessica Robyn Cracknell (11)
Milstead & Frinsted CE Primary School, Milstead

Survival Of The Fittest

No nature for hours,
Not even a flower,
Walking for hours,
I've got no power.

No shelter for miles,
This is suicidal,
Can't do this much longer,
Don't know if I'm stronger.

Just a breeze,
Will make me drop to my knees,
I see a town not too far,
But the best thing there is probably a broken down car.

I've arrived in the town,
I should be proud,
But all there is
Are some shops and a pound.

I go in to scavenge,
Then I hear a carriage,
Can I be quiet?
I think I can manage.

The carriage stops,
And I drop,
I draw my gun,
This is no fun.

Three, two, one,
It ends,
I'm done.

Kinslee Rickiel Henry (10)
Newlands Primary School, Ramsgate

Bittersweet

Sugar canes sour but my heart feels sweet,
I can feel that summer sun screaming at my feet,
Listening to the flute makes my heart skip a beat,
Because everything here you can eat,
Here in Candyland, imagination is the key,
For in Candyland anything can be,
The blackcurrant gumdrops are as sun-kissed as the sea,
Succulent sweets so sugary,
Starburst sugar canes but no savoury,
But how I could eat a burger with fries,
"Come on now, open your eyes."

Jamie Drew Blake (11)
Newlands Primary School, Ramsgate

A Footballer's Dream

I see the fans cheering my name,
I feel determined to win the game,
Me and my team are playing Liverpool,
No slide tackle, that's the rule!

Running faster than a cheetah,
Dreaming of my favourite pizza - margherita,
Feeling apprehensive, I take the ball,
Dribbling it, I nearly fall.

Bustling through the crowds,
I score a goal and the team are proud,
Feeling auspicious, I earn a new role,
What a dream, that wasn't dull!

Neil Cunningham (11)
Newlands Primary School, Ramsgate

A Whole New World

All around me
I can see
Animals hopping
Fish are bopping.

Tantalising doors made of fudge
Hard toffee sweets that won't budge
Gargantuan chimneys made of succulent cake
Candyfloss windows that you don't bake.

What a tranquil place to be
Sweets galore and animals to see
Keep dreaming until the light can be seen
And until the sun beams.

Ryan Whitworth-Saker (11)
Newlands Primary School, Ramsgate

A Footballer For The Day

Getting nervous,
Going to Russia,
Time to win this match,
Say to the team, "We can do this!"

Just believe, believe, believe,
Time to get in position,
Game starting in five, four, three, two, one,
Run, run, run,
Pass, pass, pass.

People cheering,
We've scored a goal,
What an idealistic dream this is.

Esmae Franks (11)
Newlands Primary School, Ramsgate

A World Of Art

Unicorns painting with bright horns,
Tantalising doughnuts flying around,
Water dancing around in my cup,
Pictures displayed of animals.

The sound of a roller on my sculpture,
Scratch, squidge, squash,
Laminating machine,
Click, click, click,
Alarm clock,
Ring, ring.

Veja Razukeviciute (11)
Newlands Primary School, Ramsgate

My Sweet, Sweet Home

My sweet, sweet home
My sweet, sweet home
I dream of my sweet, sweet home

Lounging on my marshmallow chair
Whilst I constantly glare
At my large candy flower
Before I go to my candy cane shower

My sweet, sweet home
My sweet, sweet home
I dream of my sweet, sweet home

Of course if I want a snack
I can go to my side shack
And if I need a drink
I can go to my chocolate sink

My sweet, sweet home
My sweet, sweet home
I dream of my sweet, sweet home.

Kai Gardiner (11)
Park Way Primary School, Maidstone

The Sweet Nightmare

Once upon a dream
A pink, shimmering sky
Cotton candy clouds
And marvellous unicorns flying above
Twinkling rainbow stars
Dancing in the night sky
And tiny elves jumping
From snow-white clouds.

The big, bright moon
Sits high in the sky
Smiling down on me
Bang, bang, bang
You hear it again
Bang, bang, bang
The dragons comes out to play

Elves jumping off the
Cotton candy clouds
Unicorns falling down
One by one
The big, bright moon
Frowning down on all of us
As the twinkling stars start
To lose sparkle

The sweet dream
Turns into a nightmare.

Ozge Ekinci (11)
Park Way Primary School, Maidstone

My Crazy Dream

Once upon a dream
A very crazy dream

The Olympic sign was high
High up in the sky

My hair got tugged and pulled
Twisted, formed and pinned

Once upon a dream
A very crazy dream

My feet hit the ground
The competition ground

The hoop twisted and turned
I twisted, leapt and spun

The crowd cheered and screamed
As I received my award.

Ivana Paynavelova (10)
Park Way Primary School, Maidstone

A Crazy, Crazy Dream

I once had a dream
A crazy, crazy dream
I swam with mermaids
Twisting and turning

I once had a dream
A crazy, crazy dream
Fairies flew around
Sparkling fairy dust

I once had a dream
A crazy, crazy dream
I swung through trees
With bright pink monkeys

I once had a dream
A crazy, crazy dream
It was only a dream
But what a crazy, crazy dream.

Grace BIshop (10)
Park Way Primary School, Maidstone

Dream Of Being Upside Down!

It's upside down in Dreamland
The sky is as green as an emerald and the floor is covered in clouds
Birds cheep at your feet and...
You see people upside down and the trees are upside down
The aeroplanes are beyond your feet
The helicopters fly beyond your feet.

Bernards Brasas (11)
Park Way Primary School, Maidstone

All About Dreams

D reams are incredible
R eal memories can be any type of dream
E njoy your dreams while they last
A dream is sometimes a happy memory
M aybe a sad dream
S o all that matters is that you're happy.

Alyssa Osborne (10)
Park Way Primary School, Maidstone

The Magical Orb

The magical orb holds heaven in your sleep
The magical orb is the end of a storm in the dull sky
The magical orb is gravity
The magical orb is deep in your heart, beating
The magical orb is the last wave through the sea
The magical orb is fire struck by lightning
The magical orb is dragon breath
The magical orb is a meteor approaching Earth
The magical orb is the end of the rainbow
The magical orb is the centre of a diamond
The magical orb is moon rock shining in the sun
The magical orb is snake venom
The magical orb is your imagination
The magical orb is the first star
The magical orb is Earth
The magical orb is yours
The magical orb is your reflection: a mirror
The magical orb is everything!

Samuel Woolley (8)
Snodland CE Primary School, Snodland

The Surfing Sharks

When I close my eyes and go to sleep
All my dreams begin to creep
But the most peculiar dream
Maybe a bit more ridiculous than it seems
It's the surfing sharks
Not the breakdancing larks

Have you ever seen anything more entertaining
Than surfing while it's raining?
One shark twirls in the air
While one really doesn't care
All the judges give the highest point score
While the crowd gives an almighty roar

Sorry sharks, it's time for me to go
But I enjoyed my seat in the front row
As my time comes to an end
I will reflect on the dream that drives me around the bend
It is time to wake up
And I will always think, hey dudes, what's up?

Noah Taylor (9)
Snodland CE Primary School, Snodland

Starlight

S tarlight shine bright
T ake me through a door tonight
A t first, I see a beautiful mermaid shimmering
R ight before my very eyes
L ots of glistening stars surround her, listening to her sing
I sla the mermaid is playing 'catch a shooting star'
G olden hair flowing everywhere
H er friends have come to join us: Crystal, Pearl, Amber and Abby
T ime to wake up, I've had a lovely dream, see you all tonight.

Chloe Theobald (7)
Snodland CE Primary School, Snodland

Fairy Tale

F riday we were walking in the woods
A lannah and I lost the dog
I spotted sparkling glitter from the bushes
R eaching out, I saw five sparkling fairies
Y ellow, red and green of the sparkling fairy wings

T here, the fairies hovered around, they left pixie dust
A ll around the sky
L eading back through the forest, the fairies and my dog
E xcited and surprised the fairies came to my rescue.

Laila Barton (8)
Snodland CE Primary School, Snodland

Dreaming Silently

Sleeping silently, my dream was awoke
Was it real or was it fake?
I stepped forwards to see a shadow near
Was it a monster? It wasn't clear
There in front of me were four hooves
Who would make the first moves?
Then I could see
Eyes staring at me
It wasn't taking me somewhere near
What could I hear, what could I hear?
Clattering sounds up all the mounds
Suddenly, my eyes opened wide
Should I hide?

Charlotte Elizabeth Tricker (8)
Snodland CE Primary School, Snodland

Connie And The Unicorn

U nicorns are pretty from top to bottom
N ever give up, even when things are hard
I t's good to believe in unicorns because your wishes may come true
C ome to the land of unicorns and see one for yourself
O ver the skies they fly and they may grant you a wish
R ead all about unicorns so you know more about unicorns
N ever quit on unicorns as you may have bad luck, I love unicorns!

Chelsea Rae Goodayle (8)
Snodland CE Primary School, Snodland

Wembley

I am standing at Wembley playing left mid
My opponent comes near me, I'm trying to get rid
Ball comes over, he goes for my shins
I kick it over his head and put it top bins
I'm so nervous, the score is one all
My mate's on the wing, he crosses the ball
Southgate's shouting and cheering my name
I score a header, winning the game.

Ryley Daniel Chance (7)
Snodland CE Primary School, Snodland

The Dinosaur Dream Tamer

Dreaming sleepily in my bed
Dinosaurs roaming around my head
A different world I see with my eyes
When I am hiding in a brilliant disguise
My imagination is weird to see
When all of the dinosaurs are chasing me
When I turn around they all scatter away
But this dream always makes my day
Riding my dinosaurs the whole entire day
Running down a pathway with all of them in a cage
Riding on a mosasaur with my scuba gear on
Then I'm going under, into the very scary depths
1,000 metres underwater there is so much to see
Then I see a megalodon and he eats me
Waking up, scared as can be
Where are the dinosaurs, where can they be?
But they are waiting in my head for me
I am going back to sleep
Where all of the dinosaurs are roaring and growling
But all of the dinosaurs are coming for me.

AJ Ashton Volbrecht (11)
St Katherine's School & Nursery, Snodland

The 10:45 To The Moon

'Twas a cold, cold winter's night
Chilly and nice
Sky black like a thick inky splodge
Snow danced in the breeze by the silhouettes of trees
Whilst the moon glistened with excitement
I lay on my bed, thoughts rushed through my head
My radiator breathing flames
When a strange scratchy sound startled me!
I sat up to attention and glanced at my door
For the strange scratchy sound I could hear no more
All that I could hear was my model steam train circling around my carpeted floor
My windows lit up with bright, shimmering lights
Followed by a horn, *beep! Beep!*
I jumped out of my skin and asked myself, "What is the need for all this din?"
I paced to the window and gasped in joy
For outside I could see a shiny red rose bus on the other side of the street!
Racing outside with my frozen feet
I hopped on the bus and found a seat
For the bus set off zooming faster and faster
Down the road as the driver boomed with laughter
When out of the blue the wheels set ablaze

Blurring my vision with a smokey haze!
As the ashy clouds cleared, my view became clear
We were floating, we were floating, we were gliding through the air
Next stop, the moon, the bus driver glared
I stared out of the window with confusion
"This is fake surely!
This is an illusion!"
Then I became dizzy, weak and truly dazed
My vision began to blur and my voice began to slur
Beep! Beep! went my alarm
I woke up, cool and calm.

Dean Brewster (11)
St Katherine's School & Nursery, Snodland

Hope's Dream

Last night when I was asleep, I walked through the glimmering, glistening portal into an enchanted, magical land
Where do you think my dream took me?
It was picturesque in Dreamland
An intricate, colossal ice house stood tall and proud in the whistling wind.

A beautiful, mesmerising ice staircase led to the gobsmacking palace that was so carefully designed
And had helter-skelter-like slides twirling out of the side
Peculiar pixies and fairies bounced around playfully whilst the candyfloss trees danced elegantly in the wind
The welcoming sign, that was meant to be pinned between two gargantuan trees, skidded along the smooth marble-like floor
But surely there couldn't be more!

Slowly, a gorgeous, stunning unicorn leant down to the edible, appetising grass and grazed elegantly
Scattered in the fields, bubblegum and strawberry-flavoured mushrooms grew every second
In the distance, a huge sign read, *Just follow your dreams!*
That is exactly what you should do

Last night, when I was asleep, I walked through the glimmering, glistening portal into an enchanted, magical land
Where do you think my dream took me?

Hope (11)
St Katherine's School & Nursery, Snodland

The Wildest Dreams

Many of the wildest dreams
On a long, beautiful sunlight beam
Wonderful dreams going through my head
Whilst I lie there engulfed by my bed
With the lids on my very blue eyes
Under each lid
A thin dream is slid
And spreads to a picture inside
A new one to explore there
Most crazy and rare
There I am standing…
Right in front of me, a UFO landing
Watching the greatest beasts
Enjoying themselves with a midnight feast
Gulping down a very plump turkey
With the sky above them so dark and murky
The king sitting on a marble chair
Right above Guy Fawkes' lair
I dream to be the very best
To climb Mount Everest.
I wish to lift the World Cup
But it will be very tough.
I will have to score lots of goals
To let the tournament unfold

And then finally touch the glorious gold
And ride in the moonlight...
Beep! Beep! sounds my alarm
Then I wake up not very calm.

Harry Attwater (11)
St Katherine's School & Nursery, Snodland

Dream To Dream

Dreams are weird ones
They always leave you muddled
They always leave you lost
Or sometimes very puzzled
My crazy story begins on a summer's night
Sometimes leaving me weirded out
And sometimes in quite a fright

First I have a pair of wings
And a winged tail!
Until I plunge into total darkness
And land in a fighter jet
Without a harness
I dodge a plane with a death wish and darkness again
That is kinda hellish!

And then I'm in Dino World
I never liked Jurassic World!
And the darkness for the third time
I open my eyes and what do I see?
Sea! I see sea!
All around me!
And I am on a battleship
The enemy's beside me
And the cannons fire

And the enemies flee
"Hurrah!" go the men
As all of it fades away
And I wake up in my bed.

Ethan Thomas Harewood (11)
St Katherine's School & Nursery, Snodland

Sleep Paralysis

I couldn't move when I awoke
I heard some words but no one spoke
I saw a figure in the corner of my eye
My stomach began to tie
The odd figure came closer to me
As it did, I saw it was a he
Some trees outside tapped on the glass
And slowly my fear began to pass
The figure was now over me
His hollow black eyes resembled the sea
He had a hunched back and slender arms
It was then I realised I had sweaty palms
His skin was as black as my cat
His eyes were black holes and he wore a hat
Bang! I heard in the hallway
I could finally move but didn't know what to say
The figure was gone and all was calm
And I was glad that I had no harm
"It was just a dream," I whispered to myself
Perhaps next time I'll dream about an elf.

Keira Rhiannon Montaner (11)
St Katherine's School & Nursery, Snodland

The Dream Worlds

There are new worlds in our dreams
In distant galaxies, the brightness gleams
Mythical lands with big and small beasts
Old castles that have gigantic feasts
Volcanic eruptions are very rare
As there are new worlds everywhere
Dinosaurs with sharp claws
Cute lions with little paws
Planes are gliding and flying
In gigantic wars, people are dying
The first people on the moon
All the dreams are fading too soon
Gigantic mansions with very tall towers
Nightmares as scary as pitch-black night, then people are fainting
Some people are having fun painting
Unfortunate people are being fried
By an alien who turns them into a pie
Then the dream is very small
I can suddenly see my bedroom wall
There are new worlds in our dreams.

Thomas Benjamin Curley (11)
St Katherine's School & Nursery, Snodland

Fantasy Dream

Dreams, dreams, dreams
I'm dreaming of a fantasy world
Cauliflowers float in sticky, runny, melted cheese
Unicorns eat their soft, fluffy candyfloss like they have been starved for days

A, B and C ride a phoenix over the sheer, treacherous hills
Jack and Jill finally succeed in getting the water from the well
Little Red Riding Hood is off again to get Grandma some pills

Beautiful, smooth-faced mermaids splash around
Because the best mer-team has just won the mer-cup
The Cyclopses have a loud game of chess
Intelligent, wise wizards zoom around on their broomsticks like witches attacking a city

I wake up finally, looking around
To hear not a sound
No wizards or unicorns or lively mermaids
Where did my dream take me?

James Morris (11)
St Katherine's School & Nursery, Snodland

Beth's Dream

Last night when I was sound asleep
Where do you think my dream took me?
Jelly cars and yoghurt cars all driving around crazily
Chocolate tree houses, I was in shock of all that I could see

Marshmallow trampolines with twice the bounce I'd ever seen
A caramel, creamy pool, golden brown like a summer tan
This was by far the most wonderful place I'd ever been

Haribo houses sat elegantly, sugary and sweet
Bubblegum and strawberry mushrooms grew off the grass constantly
Cheerful, smiley shopkeepers were lovely people to meet
Sparkling candy canes marked the entrance to the thrilling-looking theme park

I woke up, realising it was just a dream
Last night when I was sound asleep
Where do you think my dream took me?

Bethany Kate Loveland (11)
St Katherine's School & Nursery, Snodland

The Dark Side Of The Moon

Boom! The flames danced in the wind
The pitch-black side of the moon was waiting for me
The bangs, booms and zooms of the rocket kept me waiting
My friend kept on painting
Others were puzzled
I was very muddled
What was waiting for us
On the dust

The rocket went up into the inky black sky
Honestly why?
Volcanic eruptions were rare
Even though rockets were everywhere
Mythical creatures were there
But where?

Thump! The rocket touched the rocks
Then I reached into my pocket
And saw my dinosaur claw and little lion paws
Then I heard some roars
One by one they faded away
Will they come again?
I will never know what was there
Maybe dinosaurs.

Cooper Idle (10)
St Katherine's School & Nursery, Snodland

Dreams Are Fun

Dreams are fun, dreams are creative
Come and explore Dreamland with me
Come on, why are you waiting?
Are you scared, are you excited?
Let's find out in Dreamland
In Dreamland there are cotton candy clouds
In Dreamland the grass is strawberry laces
At night it's fun, isn't it?
The streams are chocolate fudge
The trees are toffee and apple Refreshers
Let's continue on
The houses are gingerbread with icing
The train is made of cake
Fantastic, let's go and discover more
The fences are made from jellybeans
The driveways are made of chocolate fingers
Why don't we stay for more?
The roses are made of sprinkles
You have to go, oh no
See you next time then.

Elisha Pickup (10)
St Katherine's School & Nursery, Snodland

Pool Party

The mansion is as big as 200 acres of pure meadow
The pool is as refreshing as a cold drink on a hot day
Friends were sitting by the edge of the pool, watching the golden, mesmerising sunset
While drinking Fanta, Tango and Vimto

Friends were watching the World Cup final while relaxing in the hot tub
The joy and relief when England won 4-3 against Germany
The happiness in Gareth Southgate's eyes when Harry Kane took the penalty and scored in the most majestic way possible
Which made the score 4-3

The chanting of England was music to our ears
The national anthem was played once more
It hadn't been played since 1966
The players celebrated and kissed the cup which made friends cry with joy.

Sean Cardiff Keefe (10)
St Katherine's School & Nursery, Snodland

The Land Of Delusional Dreams

Thoughts rushing through my brain
Like a river hunting for its prey
Fairies sprinkling magic dust
Whilst unicorns play with falling snow
As I come out of my sweetie-covered house
Which is made out of rainbow bricks and three beautifully decorated cakes
Which represent the stairs and a hard toffee door
With lollipops evenly spread all around
I see the Queen of Dreams having her royal feast
With the King of Nightmares who wants the land to be full of beasts
His lethal scream makes me shake and shudder
Which wakes me from my slumber
The fairy godmother usually puts us back to our dreams
But I'm now awake and can't get back to sleep.

Shennai Hall (11)
St Katherine's School & Nursery, Snodland

Dreamland

In Dreamland everything is wild
A seventy-year-old man playing like a child
Money growing on trees
With solid gold leaves where the weather is always mild
It usually rains cotton wool
And 100-year-old men dancing like fools
Poor people eating humongous feasts
Rich people left with the very least
You can find ten centimetre tigers in your house
But outside there is a one metre mouse
Bang! Bang! Bang! As emerald-green leaves fall to the ground
And the grass shines like the colour of the Queen's crown
Then all of a sudden you wake up to the bell of Big Ben
Wondering if your dream will ever end.

Jake Gillett-Ward (11)
St Katherine's School & Nursery, Snodland

Dream A Dream

On a long starbeam
A secret mission runs down from the midnight skies
To Malco Dread
Fast asleep in his bed
With his lids on his pretty green eyes
A thin dream slides into his mind
And spreads a picture inside

A new world right there
All held in secret software
Something that was once your bed
Could turn into something you dread
Rivers and rocks
And a treasure box
All the dreams you can dream

Every night I dream away
Only to be seen once
My dreams are happy
Some sad
But in the end
Everyone dreams a different dream every day
Maybe some carry on.

Alfie Thomas Moss (11)
St Katherine's School & Nursery, Snodland

Dreams

Shimmering in the distance, the stars glisten like intricate diamonds
The acres of enchanted galaxy await before my eyes
And the vast range of planets orbit the scorching sun

Floating beside me, my limbs have a mind of their own
As a whole new world is being shown
And the sight of rockets blows my mind

Astonishing creatures roam planets
As fantasy takes over and creates a racket
I meet a kind-hearted fellow that is neon yellow
And hold its hand, walking through a meadow

I gradually disappear and let go of its hand
As I come back to reality
I begin once again to walk on land.

Millie (11)
St Katherine's School & Nursery, Snodland

The House

As you approach
Rotting walls and smashed windows
Creaking from footsteps that were never there
Screams in the dead of night

Drip goes the rusty tap
Bang from the falling pipes
Every step closer could cost your life
A dead body lies stretched, fresh blood pouring out onto the floor

Eyeballs litter the shelves
Whilst bodies scatter the floor
You can never make it out alive
Everything goes dark

Pounding on the big oak door
There is no escape
The ghost appears in its former glory
Towering above
The end is here, this is the end.

Isabella N (11)
St Katherine's School & Nursery, Snodland

Legendary Galaxy Party!

D ancing and prancing, Penny, Oso and Lamby are dancing above the galaxy
R ed fireworks burning through the legendary sky as Mr Snuggles is enjoying himself at this wonderful party
E njoying this magical experience for the first time
A stonishing speakers burst their eardrums as they can't stop dancing
M arshmallo is kicking some beats in his DJ booth, with his cross-eyed mask
"I magine anything," Marshmallo says, "it will appear someday!"
N ever stop dreaming, just keep going and dream
G o and enjoy your spectacular dreams!

Madison Wainwright (10)
St Katherine's School & Nursery, Snodland

Candyland

Marshmallow clouds make me proud
Syrup lake, a rich cow, chocolate trees and fluffy bees
Whoosh goes the strawberry rocket
Fruit Lockets in my pocket
Sour leaves and honey bees make me feel very pleased
Candyfloss sheep, Pancake Pete
Hot chocolate rivers don't make me shiver
Will always surround the candy kingdom
Which is pleasured with freedom

Now the time is winter
Tables have turned
Gummy bears are heading to Pancake Pete's party

While the time passes by
Candyfloss sheep start to fly
So I say goodbye, until another night.

Billy Moody (10)
St Katherine's School & Nursery, Snodland

Mythical Forest

As I quietly strolled through the mythical forest
The brightly-coloured rainbow shone down
I slowly crept into the mesmerising cave
To find an elegant unicorn combing its soft, shiny hair
The baby dinosaurs danced in the pouring rain
Whilst the beautiful birds chirped merry tunes

The delicate fairies floated in the crystal clear sky
As the wild flowers bloomed by the side of the river bend
The dreamy mermaids slowly sank into the baby blue river

Dwarves mined away at the grey marble rocks to find the gems
Whilst the narwhals chilled in the bubbly hot tub.

Tilly-Marie Turgoose (11)
St Katherine's School & Nursery, Snodland

My Fantasy Dream

I woke up in a dream
I found myself in a tower
I sat up in my bed
And felt a waft of power
I stood up and saw
Waiting in front of me
The Cheshire Cat
"Come and see!"
He grabbed my hand
He took me away
We fell down a slide
Made of hay
We swam in a pool
Made of jelly
We ate our way through
And filled up our bellies
We went past Humpty Dumpty
Who fell off a wall
And went past Winnie the Pooh
With a honey ball
Jack and Jill were on the swings
And Snow White was by the birds
Where she always sings.

Grace (11)
St Katherine's School & Nursery, Snodland

Playing For Tottenham

A strange little dream
On one pitch
Twenty-two people
And a full stand of fans

Playing at Tottenham's new stadium
The best club debut you could ask for
This is where dreams come true
On the ball, dribbling at defenders

The sound of the chant
Of proud fans cheering on their team
To follow legends
Or take Tottenham to the Champions League

A new life full of fame and glory
Bringing home trophies galore
Tottenham could finally win the prem
As a legend for Tottenham
I wake, the future may never be found...

Oscar Miles (11)
St Katherine's School & Nursery, Snodland

Time Travel Into The Future

A million dreams can come true
I went to bed last night
And I dreamed
About time travelling into the future
I dreamed about all of the birthdays
I dreamed about all of the sad times
That made happy times
I dreamed about who I would marry
And if I would have any children
And if they would be a boy or a girl

Then I woke up and I realised
That a dream can come true
But only if you believe and don't give up
Embrace your dream
I admit it may not be easy
But you can make a dream
And a million dreams can come true.

Olivia Nash Thompson (11)
St Katherine's School & Nursery, Snodland

Magical Dreams

D reams can be very magical if you believe
R acing through your head like a racing car winning first place
E nchanted forests, creatures and lots more for you to see
A ll waiting for you to tell on one special day, just you wait and see what your dreams will be
M ake the impossible possible, anything can happen
I n your stunning place you will find and see new things you never knew existed
N ow it's your time to shine and dream anything you wish
G et your dreaming hat on and think of something very magical.

Chloe (11)
St Katherine's School & Nursery, Snodland

The Panda And The Fox

There's a nervous feeling in the living room
The ceiling is as red as a ruby
The walls are as brown as bark
A small panda sits on the dark blue leather sofa
He watches TV like a cat on a hunt
The Lotto results are next
Smash is the noise the window makes when the large grey fox jumps in
It twists and swirls and hangs from the light
Its tail swinging violently
Eventually, it screeches and leaves the town
Panda's mouth lets out a sigh of relief
He's missed the results
It's back to the broom for him.

Ciaran Oliver-Jones (11)
St Katherine's School & Nursery, Snodland

Dreamland

Everything is different in Dreamland
People sleep in clouds with beds of non-sticky candyfloss
And unicorns of multicolours fly by daily
The sun smiles at us every morning
And birds sing their beautiful songs
In the summer butterflies, fly through walls
And in the winter, snowflakes fall from below and above
Children play with their friends all year round
And they zoom rapidly through the sky, dodging aeroplanes
Everything is wonderful in Dreamland
And when I open my eyes in the morning
I never want to leave.

Maria May Bowyer (11)
St Katherine's School & Nursery, Snodland

Entering My Nightmare

A black tile path
Leading to my fears
A gloomy, eerie mansion waiting for me
It's ghost-infested
Full of cobwebs
It hasn't been cleaned in years!

Splash! An unrecognisable goo drips from the ceiling
Eagles squawking
Blackbirds chirping
The moon smirking down
Stars that turn evil!

I enter with my mouth gaping
Creaking floorboards
Moving objects
An unpleasant surprise!
The aroma of an old, dusty house
Makes me choke!

Brooke Amy Urbanowicz (11)
St Katherine's School & Nursery, Snodland

The Endgame

D uring the huge, dangerous war on a dark, gloomy night, the Avengers were fighting like there was no tomorrow

R apidly, Captain Marvel flew across the gigantic ship like a meteorite and destroyed it in seconds

E ventually, the sun peeked out from the horizon while the war was happening

A mazingly, Iron Man dashed to Thanos and grabbed the stones as quick as a flash

M eanwhile, Iron Man snapped his fingers strongly, but he was not strong enough to survive, so he died.

Daniel Stroud (11)
St Katherine's School & Nursery, Snodland

Topsy Turvy Dreamland

It's topsy turvy in Dreamland
The houses are made of sweets
It's summer every day
Never is there snow or rain
It's a happy place, the swimming pools are chocolate fountains
The mountains are made of gingerbread
The flowers are made of ribbons
I feel happy here
It's topsy turvy in Dreamland
Gravity doesn't apply to this place
Never is it a dangerous place
And no nightmares to be seen
And the shoelaces are made of strawberry laces.

Ben Wade (11)
St Katherine's School & Nursery, Snodland

Lost In The Forest

As I walk through the white snow
Something starts to glow
I walk towards it
It stops, I feel lost, I can't get out
I start to shout

I'm lost, there is no way out
I am stuck forever in my nightmare
I am cold outside and inside

I am scared
I don't know what to do
I can hear noises
That I don't like
It is all a big fright

There are dark skies
Snow reaches my legs and trees overlook me.

Taylor Mannerings (11)
St Katherine's School & Nursery, Snodland

I'm Dreamin'

I 'm tired
M aking dreams come true

D reaming away until the dawn of the day
R eality is a dream in disguise
E ach dream is quality
A ll you need to do is believe
M agnificent dreams can come true
I 've unravelled a lot of dreams and hope that they come true
N othing but dreams, dreams and dreams
G rowing confidence that one day my dreams will come true.

Kyle Goodall (11)
St Katherine's School & Nursery, Snodland

My Dream

As I drifted off to sleep
I took one massive leap
To arrive at Dreamland

As I walked around the place
I saw the Roman base
Preparing for battle

Butterflies were gliding around
Getting ready to land on the ground
Their beautiful wings spread out wide

I found a house
That belonged to a mouse
I was rather intrigued

Vvvvv!
My alarm bell rang
I turned it off with a bang.

Grace Wastell (11)
St Katherine's School & Nursery, Snodland

Nightmares

I lay there and shuddered
There was not one noise but another
A noise came from the radiator like thunder
Nightmares, nightmares

Oooooo!
A train came out with a boy on top
Down below in a freight carriage lay some rocks
Nightmares, nightmares

The boy ran across the white, crunchy snow
And pushed the snow back like using dough
The boy ran through the dancing wind
Nightmares, nightmares.

Chloe Annabelle Rosier (11)
St Katherine's School & Nursery, Snodland

Candyland

Chocolate trees, marshmallow bees dancing around
The sugary daisies make me pleased
Sour leaves, candyfloss sheep and syrup coming from the chocolate trees
Hot chocolate rivers don't give me shivers and will always surround the candy kingdom which is pleasured with freedom
Now the time is winter, all the gummy bears are heading to the pancake party
While the time is turning night, Candy Kingdom is saying goodbye until another night.

Kai Hayes (10)
St Katherine's School & Nursery, Snodland

Dream

D reams come true in your sleep, but only in your sleep
R emember to not tell anyone about your dreams because they may not come true
E very day you go to bed and have a nice dream, if it's bad then get a dreamcatcher
A ll you have to do is have a dream and try and make it come true, and if it does then lucky you
M emories might come true in your dream like becoming a celebrity, like Ant and Dec.

Cameron (11)
St Katherine's School & Nursery, Snodland

This Is My World

Everything is edible in Dreamland
The sky is as yummy as cotton candy
And the floor is entirely caramel
The gummy bears knock on the wafer door and offer you a hot chocolate
Down low, the gummy fishes swim
And up high, Dorito planes fly swiftly
The gingerbread houses get smaller every day
But as everything fades and my eyes open
I smile, realising that it was all just my imagination.

Sebastian Lane (10)
St Katherine's School & Nursery, Snodland

Dream

A strange little dream
On a long night
Came down from the night sky
Filling my mind with imagination and excitement

Every night I dream away
Filling my mind with vivid sights
With lots of dreams carried away
People lie there fast asleep

With a sudden surprise
They turn around and realise
That it was all a dream
And may carry on the next night.

Louise Zoe Joan Waddell (11)
St Katherine's School & Nursery, Snodland

Dream

D reams come true if you believe in them, but only when you're just asleep
R emember, don't tell a soul your dream or your dream will always be a dream
E very night a chocolate horse wakes up and gallops through a candy field
A ll you have to do is have a dream in your sleep
M aybe it's your lucky day and your best dream will come true.

Rebecca Louise Daynes (11)
St Katherine's School & Nursery, Snodland

A Wheelie Wild Dream

Last night I remember the vroom that ran through my mind
The adrenaline racing through my blood cells
The luscious smell of diesel spitting out my beautiful, metallic, silver exhaust
Everyone glancing, recording, cheering, what an incredible feeling
The sound of a two-stroke scraping, all the teens' knees knocking
I leapt over a jump the size of two monster trucks.

Izaac Sayers (11)
St Katherine's School & Nursery, Snodland

The Mind Controls Itself

Murder
Silence
No escape
The tap drips
It breaks the silence sending a shiver down my spine
It's live, the world is a simulation
Maybe it's a sign
It requests concentration
To master this game
Every step I take, my life is closer to the edge
Heart beating, lungs struggling to grab the air
I awake from the madness inside my head.

Evie-Mae Hawkins (11)
St Katherine's School & Nursery, Snodland

My Dream

Last night when I was fast asleep
Lying under my fluffy pink blanket
I had the most amazing dream
Lying in the tall, luscious, green grass
Whilst the bright yellow sun beamed down onto my tanned body
Sitting up to see the atmosphere
A beautiful colourful parrot flew down and asked me what my wish was
I woke up to realise that it was only a dream!

Skye-Olivia Harris (11)
St Katherine's School & Nursery, Snodland

The Sweet Town

Houses made of pancakes sit next to a lake of syrup
Strawberry boats float off into the marshmallow sunset
Blueberry birds fly above our heads and land in the lake
Chocolate puppies bounce on raspberry mushrooms
Gummy bunnies hop around eating the lace grass
Gingerbread houses are dotted around the sweet town.

Hollie Elizabeth Browne (10)
St Katherine's School & Nursery, Snodland

Dreams Come True

M ake sure you believe in yourself
Y our imagination can be strong

D on't discourage yourself
R eal imagination can come true
E mbrace your imagination
A ll you need to do is use your mind
M aybe today your dream will go through your head.

Mia Hamilton Greenstreet (10)
St Katherine's School & Nursery, Snodland

In A Tutu

I look down and see a tutu, beautiful and pink
I spin and spin, my tutu whirling with me

Onstage I'm alone but I feel happy and strong under the coloured lights
I finish in third position
A smile glued to my face
My hair still put tightly in a bun

The music stops, the audience get to their feet
And all the clapping and cheering
Fills my ears with joy.

Rosie Jane Layberry (9)
St Mark's CE Primary School, Tunbridge Wells

Dreamy Life

D *ash*, *bam*, I'm in my dream world
R ainbows appear here
E xotic gemstones are found
A nimals are friendly
M agical mysteries happen here
Y ippee! A palace!

L ots of shops are here
I t is wonderful
F antastic price offers
E nd of my dream has come.

Oliwia Zborowska (9)
St Mark's CE Primary School, Tunbridge Wells

WWII

When I close my eyes and sleep,
I'm comfy in my bed,
Then a whizzing, whirling, strange sensation goes on inside my head,
All I see is the deep, cruel night,
I have been betrayed by my rest,
My sleep given to darkness,
Know not whether worst or best.

Then a bright candlelight flickers,
There's a light inside my eyes,
A bang! A boom! A fizz!
Men's shouts and women's cries.
I've gone back to 1940,
Where bullets fill the air,
Bombs spark like fireworks,
Leaves and branches tear.

Then all I see is fire,
I wish I was blind again,
Heat and smoke burn my lungs,
Animals beg in their pen.
Then when I open my eyes and wake,
I'm comfy in my bed,
The whizzing, whirling strange sensation is gone from in my head.

Freya
St Martin's CE Primary School, Folkestone

My Football Dream

Running forwards down the wing,
I'm about to shoot that's the thing,
Then it happens, I hit the ball,
Hard and low like in a game of pool,
Bottom corner, in it goes,
So full of joy I strike a pose,
Winning the game,
It really ain't lame,
My team is the best,
Ten times better than the rest.
Playing for my national team,
All our trophies, they do gleam,
Then I hear someone chanting my name,
I shut my eyes enjoying the fame,
Then I open them again...
Only to see my mum stood over me,
Saying, "Come on!"
And that I'm going to be late,
And then I realise with great disappointment,
It was all merely a dream!

Hayden John Bestford (11)
St Martin's CE Primary School, Folkestone

Lost In The Galaxy

Dark, gloomy, surrounding the night,
Stars bright, lighten the darkness,
Lonely, sad, despair, fright,
Bang, crash, noise all day long.

Yesterday, adventure, running, walking,
Always dark, silent as night,
Shooting stars, so bright, constantly talking,
As they jump over my head.

Today, I will enjoy the moment,
As there is no way to live the moment again,
Joyful, full of excitement,
For I will conquer today as no other.

Tomorrow, I will travel past purple and blue,
Happiness, enjoyment will sprint down my spine,
No sadness, no sorrow, it will all disintegrate too,
As I explore for one time and one time only.

Katie Harris (11)
St Martin's CE Primary School, Folkestone

My Mermaid Dream

Ocean as wonderful as chocolate,
Sand gold and water blue,
A tail instead of a foot,
Purple scales too.

Gliding through the water,
A terrible sight I see,
My dolphin friend, they've caught 'er!
And a net on top of me.

Thrusting my tail around,
I'm tangled like bed hair!
But the net only weighs a pound,
Being free is my only care.

Bang! I hit the side of the boat,
I think, *it's what they deserved*,
Then go to take off my dolphin's net coat,
The dent in the metal monster, curved.

Return to the depths I shall,
Swimming in the H20,
Never needing a towel,
I watch my friend go.

Jessica Wright (10)
St Martin's CE Primary School, Folkestone

Dreaming May Come True

I dreamed I was a footballer,
Best in the world,
Young and true,
Through and through.

I was number nine,
Scoring through the outside line,
Our team never lost,
Other teams had to pay the cost.

Scoring goals is what I did,
The other teams ran and hid,
A legend is what I was,
Best legend in the game.

Chelsea was my home team,
Stamford Bridge is where I played,
Blue till the day I die,
England, it was coming home.

Captain of my national team,
Striker is what I played,
Won the Euros,
And World Cup,
Won the Prem,
And FA cup,

Champions League was easy too,
I hope this dream does come true.

Michael Guiver (11)
St Martin's CE Primary School, Folkestone

Candyland

Sprinkles dancing in the air,
I find a gummy bear.
Chocolate bars melting in the sun,
I smell some nice hot cross buns.
In a land that doesn't exist,
Candyland is always a myth.
Looking around at the sweets,
While listening to the cool candy beats.
Looking up at the sky,
At the cotton candy so high.
The hot fire burns it all down,
While the candy canes come out of the ground.
Sugar paper is yummy to eat,
All the candy in the land is neat.
Candyland is the best,
It's better than the rest.

Alice Ellen Law (11)
St Martin's CE Primary School, Folkestone

The Room

The sun started to go to sleep as the moon started to rise
I saw a cracked candle-lit room in front of my eyes
Shadows started to appear with a voice in the background
This room gave me fear of what I used to dream about
I was shivering, I was cold, I was worried, I was scared
I started to hear someone say my name...
It all began to blur
Someone in the distance started to stare
The lights came on
She was still there!
She looked me in the eye...
She asked if I was scared
I closed my eyes and imagined I was not there.

Isabelle Lamb (11)
St Martin's CE Primary School, Folkestone

Candyland

The floor is made of cotton candy,
The trees are made of taffy!
There are unicorns flying in the sky,
I'm as happy as a daffodil,
I am as confused as a mouse trapped in a house,
Bright green grass with the most beautiful coloured flowers blooming from the ground below!
In Candyland all the unicorns bring you cupcakes and presents,
In Candyland if you wish for something that you want, it comes true,
In Candyland you can eat all the candy you want,
In Candyland you don't have to eat vegetables.

Seren-Mair Worrall (11)
St Martin's CE Primary School, Folkestone

Being Famous For A Day!

Cameras circling around me,
Fans chanting my name,
Light beaming in my eyes,
It was nice having that fame.

I took one step forwards,
I felt great,
I wished it wouldn't end,
Because I felt amazing!

Autographs flying through the air,
Pictures of me everywhere,
Money swarming my every look,
For I'd just published a new book.

As I finished my last line,
I felt happiness crawling down my spine,
But little did I know, I'd woken up,
And it was all a dream!

Maya Briggs (10)
St Martin's CE Primary School, Folkestone

The Fairground

The Ferris wheel spinning like a dog trying to chase after its tail,
I feel excited to ride the fast, furious roller coaster,
Whoosh!

Coconuts getting thrown to play coconut shy,
Coconut milk squirting up and splashing others,
Hook-a-duck winning a lot of prizes,
Zorbs on water.
Getting Coca-Cola.

Seeing children on the roundabout facing their fears,
With seniors on the merry-go-round,
And families on the bumper cars,
Bumping into each other.

Evie Aitchison (11)
St Martin's CE Primary School, Folkestone

The Forest

The wind was a lonely wolf,
A crow flew through the trees,
A cat perched on a fence nearby,
And my hair blew in the breeze.

Eerie eyes stared,
The grass began to sway,
A clown grabbed my hand,
Would I see another day?

The sun started to set,
The moon began to rise,
A candlelit hut,
Perched before my eyes.

Thud! What was that?
I started to dread,
Loss of hope, loss of happiness,
I opened my eyes and to my relief,
I was safe at home in bed!

Izzy Taylor (11)
St Martin's CF Primary School, Folkestone

The Cat Surprise

Walking down a path,
Finding my new house,
Hopeful that there is not a mouse,
Looking at my watch,
There is no way to stop,
Jumping in, I need a nap,
Wait a sec there are cats,
Searching around,
What happened to my lucky pound?
Going down the cats' road,
While putting in the special code,
At least they are cats not rats,
Let's take a test,
Are cats the best?
Yes!

Hannah Hollows (10)
St Martin's CE Primary School, Folkestone

The Portal Clown

The clock strikes midnight,
I'm lying in bed, full of fright,
The rain hammers on my windows,
My door creaks like a crow.

My wall glows red,
I'm going to get out of bed,
It is shining in my room,
Is this thing about to create doom?

White face pokes through,
Red hair too,
A little red nose,
It isn't holding a rose...

Jack Rolfe (10)
St Martin's CE Primary School, Folkestone

The Goat In A Boat

As I walked across the crooked bridge,
I heard something humming like a fridge.
I saw a goat in a boat hovering above my head!
The mist pushed the goat into the distance,
As the goat tried to stay afloat.
Boom went the goat, it landed flat on my head!
As I went to bed, I saw a goat in a boat.

Morgan Baker-Goode (11)
St Martin's CE Primary School, Folkestone

Dragon

D agger-like teeth
R aging with fumes
A nger, knocking down a tower in the distance
G reat ferocious claws ripping straw off houses
O blong, pointed horns terrorising people living in fear
N ever caring who he kills...

Rohan Syred (11)
St Martin's CE Primary School, Folkestone

Wind

Swaying trees all day long,
As the birds sing a lovely song.
Children playing in the sun,
Spreading joy, bringing fun.

As the flowers wave hello,
A child comes with a pretty bow.
As it falls from her hair,
It dances through the air.

Hayley Conley (11)
St Martin's CE Primary School, Folkestone

Autumn Dream

Swaying grass.
Falling berries.
Stepping through.
Soaring swings.

Dawdling clouds.
Fretting birds.
Drifting wind.
Doodling plane.

Whispering trees.
Fussing leaves.
Wishing willows.
Wandering squirrels.

Mollie Coughlan (11)
St Martin's CE Primary School, Folkestone

Football Pitch

Football pitch
Loud noise!
Swaying grass
Players making their pass.
Wind and rain
Makes a dirty game.
Once again
So much pain!
Rushing to the goal
That goal is so big.

Jack Tumber (10)
St Martin's CE Primary School, Folkestone

Horrorland

Headteacher, headteacher gives me an idea
You know you're not a preacher but you are a teacher of my old preacher
I see a light, I see light way in the dark
Mrs Seymour has just been taken by a lark
"My child, my child, I'll see you in the whispers
Listen to the sound of your faith
Horrorland, Horrorland awaits you right down your lane."
Will it be small? Will it be big? I don't know
But oh no! My wig!
Yay Mr Stringer's here with one of his tarts
I don't really like it but it's a piece of art
I take a bite, it goes spinning
Oh, we're at school, wow, that was a scene
Well that is it, we'll see you again at the old town
Lark's Ark!

Chimamanda Kaitlyn Afam (8)
St Peter & St Paul Catholic Primary Academy, St Paul's Wood Hill

You Are Your Dreams

You are your dreams
Your dreams are yours
No one will take your dreams
You will arrive at your dreams
You drive your dreams
Your heart will take you to your dreams
No one can take your dreams
No one can stop your dreams
You are your dreams
Focus on your dreams
No one can take your dreams
No one can change your dreams
Aim for your dreams
Go with your heart
Go with your mind
Go with love
Go with life
Go with ambition
Go with your dreams
Go with your dreams.

Esen Arif (10)
St Peter & St Paul Catholic Primary Academy, St Paul's Wood Hill

Lost

Where am I?
Abandoned in the dark
Who on Earth would leave me here
Scratching my faint mark?

Look around, what do I see?
Nothing is in my sight
Trying to hold back my tears
I look for something bright

Plain lost, nothing to see
I think of something to do
Though I can't see my hands
I fiddle with my left shoe

I'm awoken by a noise
And give a sign of relief
My nightmare is now over
I stop the chattering of my teeth.

Lucy Chisom Ekpe (10)
St Peter & St Paul Catholic Primary Academy, St Paul's Wood Hill

Dream

Once upon a dream
In a faraway land
A potion spilled
It created something grand

As a young child snored
Ivy climbed the walls
The dark green leaves crinkled
As whales beckoned their calls

Tucked away in a warm, fluffy cloud
She resisted the urge to say her dreams aloud
Floating around in the starry night sky
She looked down as she began to fly

Her eyes opened
Her dream ended
Everything was mush
As if it had been blended.

Isabelle Winkley (11)
St Peter & St Paul Catholic Primary Academy, St Paul's Wood Hill

The Monster Is Freaking Me Out!

What is it that I got?
It feels like something is getting steeper
It's scaring me a lot
I hear something like a stair creeper!

It sounds like a scary cat
And the wind blows something like hair
The freaky sound is like a bat
And the roaring sound of a bear!

It gives me a thing
I think I have to give a leap
It's a sound of a buzzing wing
Why do you do something like a creep?
Who is it?
Monster!

Maria Barbashova (9)
St Peter & St Paul Catholic Primary Academy, St Paul's Wood Hill

Monsters

Monsters hairy, monsters scare
Monsters hide just anywhere
Under your bed, in your head, in your bin
Until your mum comes in

Gloopy green and rarely seen
Big red spots and small white dots
Scaresome glowing teeth
Skin that's like raw beef

If you peek
You smell a reek
Under your bed
He rests his head
Let me say one more thing
Don't give your monster a ring.

Isabelle Keely Jones (11)
St Peter & St Paul Catholic Primary Academy, St Paul's Wood Hill

Fortnite

There are a lot of guns and you need to run
You will not have fun
Now let's talk about wins and skins
First I have lots of wars
And skins and moves
The good skin is Galaxy
The best move is Chicken Dance
The best guns are the Boom Bow and Heavy Sniper
The best vehicle is the Driftboard because you can no scope like crazy

There is lots of money in the V-Bucks Bunny
There used to be a storm breaker
Iron Man gloves were just Aimbot
Captain America's shield does 275 damage
And the Infinity Gauntlet does 300
You'd better watch out for Thanos, he will destroy all eternity
Don't get your hopes up, you may not win
You may not get some skins
You definitely need some pickaxes and don't forget some Back Bling for adventures or pets
So get a win and have some fun!

Joshua J (9) & Alfie M
St Peter's CE Primary School, Folkestone

My Worst Nightmare

In the misty night
There stands a metal knight
His shining armour makes it bright
Beware for a freaky fright

There are whispers in the air
You'd better prepare
For a spooky funfair
Come in if you dare

The doors are slowly opening
They make a tiny creak
There inside we can see a very big leak

We follow the trail
And our dogs bail
And we have failed
We see a clown

We fall through a trap
There is no map
We can't escape
It is the end of the day

We wake, our faces all frightened
We go downstairs

And there we see a very big leak
Could our dream really be... true?

Marika S (9) & Brandon
St Peter's CE Primary School, Folkestone

Banana Friend

I went on a roller coaster
And brought a poster
I met my friends
And I didn't want the day to end
We met a banana
That was a professional dancer
We found out his name was Bob
And we accidentally called him Log
He bounced around like a dog
The roller coaster sounded like a whoosh
The roller coaster broke down
So we went to town
We bought a pizza
It was better than chocolate at Easter
We went to the park
And the trees were made out of bark
We met Jojo
With her pet Bow Bow
The banana scared us
On the bus.

Emma Longley (8) & Emily-Rose Middleton
St Peter's CE Primary School, Folkestone

Dreaming Of Paradise!

An eight-storey hotel with a motel next door
A pool as shiny as Mr G's head
I felt like a hot tomato (probably because I was as tanned as a potato)
The dream started to change
Soon I saw a crane that I hope I never see again!
Then I saw a horse's mane and I ate a candy cane
Then I saw the queen's pain
I had a secret base with a pencil case
Then I had a race at the end of the day
I had to pay
I hate to say
Someone had died.

Olivia Sullivan (9), Kyle Horgan & Oscar J (8)
St Peter's CE Primary School, Folkestone

Platform 9¾

One day, we get a letter
We don't know what do to
It makes us feel better
Then we go *moo!*

Then we go to platform 9¾
And we meet Kreacher
Not the train that goes to three daughters
We were supposed to meet a teacher

Then we get another letter
It tells us to go home
It says it's for the better
And we fly back to the dome.

Jayden Michael J (8) & Sonny Haydn King
St Peter's CE Primary School, Folkestone

Hamsters!

I am a hamster as keen as can be
I love my cage, how lovely it can be
I love my sister and she is called Amelia

Once I met a friend called Banana Face
Then I packed a suitcase
Because I was travelling to Ace
I went on a boat with a goat

I met Mr Goodeal by the Eiffel Tower
Then I got some power
I got trapped in my cage!

Ruby EC (8)
St Peter's CE Primary School, Folkestone

The Zoo Full Of Magic

Last night at twilight
No street lights in sight
The zoo was clear
Then something appeared
Flying like Dumbo
But it was jumbo
With Ron, my stupid brother
Without our mother
An elephant it was
And I walked away and said, "Soz!"
There were dancing fish
Then Ron shouted, "Sis!"

Amber J (9)
St Peter's CE Primary School, Folkestone

The Zoo Of Magic

Last night at twilight
There were no streetlights in sight
The zoo was clear
Then something appeared
Flying like Dumbo
But it was Jumbo
With Ginny my boring sister
So she said, "Mister."
An elephant it was
Ginny walked away and said sos
There were dancing fish
I called over my sis.

Leni Adelaide King (9)
St Peter's CE Primary School, Folkestone

A Tiring Tale

If I was an athlete I would run, run and run
And when the day was done
I would just sleep for one minute
Finally, the thing I'd do is play with Bob all day
And then climb a stack of fresh brown hay
Then with all my friends, we would go to the beach
And find a lot of leeches.

Betsy P-B (8)
St Peter's CE Primary School, Folkestone

Four-Legged Dinosaurs

One sunny day I went to see the dinosaurs. I saw them and I also saw a baby one. It was struggling to walk to its mother. Instead, I took care of it. I fed it until it got big. Then I had to use a stepladder to feed it. I called it Greedy because it was always hungry!

Tobias A D S Simpson (9)
St Peter's CE Primary School, Folkestone

St Peter's Rocks!

St Peter's is the best
Even in a mess
The teachers are cool
They make other teachers look cruel
The children are noisy
They're not woosy
The worship is nice
Better than ice
The lunch is yum
In my tum.

Demi Leigh D (8)
St Peter's CE Primary School, Folkestone

Running From Scared

Trees rattling in the raging winds
Suddenly there appears a wolf that grins
As the snarling wolf comes closer and closer
This gives to me a terrible fright
So I turn and I run and I run for my life
Into the distance, a castle dark and tall
With pointed steeples and high, dark walls
Now safe from the wolf, I creep through a dim lit corridor
But now what awaits me I am very unsure
As I hear footsteps of unexpected, I turn, scream and jump
Of an old man stood before me - he looks like a grump
When this old man reaches out his old hand
I fear what's in store so I scream some more
Out of the castle I run with dread
Into a graveyard, the land of the dead
My heart pounding with fear
Of what could be near
But thankfully I awake safe in my bed
Free from the dream I had in my head.

Frankie Griffin-Greca (9)
St Teresa's Catholic Primary School, Ashford

Venom Inside Me

People say it'll be okay,
But they have no idea what I suffer every day,
It's like death but it will not end,
It's like sharing minds, only you have no control,
So you can only pray that this venom will stay away,
Look outside,
The sun's blaze scorches the land,
If only I knew there's a raging storm inside me,
Its desires clawing at my life,
"Food," it goes, "hungry, kill, bite heads off and pile their bodies."
It gets in your head like a drunkenness, thirst for blood,
Think of me, a slave, host to this parasite,
It's using me, why can't I see?
It's a blindness,
Should have been dead a long time ago,
But his death will come at a cost - mine,
I'm ashamed to say we need each other,
But why me?
When it gets inside you, your life will slowly drop,
I used to have a wife, now I live at the docks,
But then I realise there is no me anymore,
There is only us,
No! No! No!

I've tried to fight this feeling, it's making me insane,
Now people run away but it's me that feels pain,
As the dark ticks away, my life is turning grey,
Tick, tock, Venom is here,
Tick, tock, your time has come,
Tick, tock, accept your fate,
You're dead already.

Noah Brooks (8)
St Teresa's Catholic Primary School, Ashford

Dancing On A Street

D ancing on the street
A nyone can follow the beat
N otes can make you wonder
C an you feel the shock of thunder?
I will dance across the rocky street
N ot one person will ignore the beat
G o on and dance but don't feel the heat

O n the grass we dance back and forth
N ot one person will stop us, so let's keep on track

A simple drink will be just fine

"S top," the guard says, "there's a very long line."
T he team members walk away when I start to dance
"R eally?" they all say while the crowd begins to prance
E xcitedly the crowd begins to dance in groups
E legantly, the members walk back like they are my troops
T hen we play kings and queens but we get tired and go home.

Sheena Ndduga (9)
St Teresa's Catholic Primary School, Ashford

Flying

F lying is amazing, it's a child's best dream, flying means you can do anything

L ying anywhere we want, sleeping in our nest, dreams come true and this world is not poop, you can do anything you want in this world of dreams

Y ou people full of dreams, finish your tea and come with me, it will be fun, trust me, it's safe as long as your dreams are and it will be amazing

I n your beds, dreaming about the thing you want, tomorrow is another day and more dreams come

N ow it's morning, Dreamworld starts, all children are welcome to share their dreams

G oing home, having dinner, wanting to go to sleep for another day in Dreamworld but dreams will always by a mystery.

Edward Badze (8)
St Teresa's Catholic Primary School, Ashford

A Funny Dream

I had a funny dream last night, it really made me laugh
I dreamt my sister, Lola, was a mermaid in the bath

She flapped her tail and swished her hair and was happy as could be
She pulled the plug out, gracious me!
And was sucked into the sea

"This is fabulous, amazing to me!" said Lola
As she was swimming with other fishes in the deep blue sea
But then my sister, Lola, got eaten by a shark
And all at once my dream turned scary, scary in the dark

Then came me, Charlie, superhero orca
There to save the day
I punched that shark so hard his insides turned to jelly
All at once my sister, Lola, plopped out of his belly.

Charlie Hall (8)
St Teresa's Catholic Primary School, Ashford

Wonderland

W onderland is the place where all your dreams come true
O n the land and in the sea, you'll never know what's new
N ever-ending thoughts and tales come from time to time
D readful ones to happy ones, all waiting in line
E ven though kids, young to old, have to go to bed
R eading and consistent games are always in their heads
L ottery tickets and Fanta drinking are all allowed in here
A nd sometimes kids scoffing sweets is all that you can hear
N o fighting, lies or injuries in this land of gold
D o come here to have a taster if you are really bold.

Nathan Deus Dedit Epulani (9)
St Teresa's Catholic Primary School, Ashford

Football For Life

When I'm older I want to be
A professional footballer in the Premier League
When I play I will be
Just as good as Lionel Messi

I soon will get the skills
Scoring on the pitch will always give me thrills
I hope that I will be an inspiration
And also get some admiration

You live a good life for a reason
And hopefully, you play in a hot season
In your life you have to believe
That there are many things to achieve

Last of all, football is fun
Kicking a ball in the glorious sun.

Solomon Olajide (9)
St Teresa's Catholic Primary School, Ashford

Creeped Out

C rawling rapidly in the dark unknown cave
R unning before I got hit by a darkness wave
E nding in a pile of rocks
E ventually holes appeared in my socks
P lanning an escape was no use
E lephants were stamping into my brain and my body felt loose
D read gradually grew on my face

O ut in the dark I tightened my shoelace
U nderneath the ground was a deep valley
T hen I realised it was endless and my fears raised to 100 on the tally...

Leon Jijo (9)
St Teresa's Catholic Primary School, Ashford

Fairies In Fairyland

I can see fairies, they are all nice so come out and play
Don't be frightened, they are nice

I am in Fairyland with you so don't be scared
I will stay because I am friendly, just like you

Don't be scared of the dark
The moon is light just like the sun
Because I am here with you

I am always with you because this is a good place
I'm really happy that you are happy always
Now it's daytime, we all can go out and play.

Molly Elizabeth James (8)
St Teresa's Catholic Primary School, Ashford

Monsters Missing

My monsters are not here tonight
It's the fairies who come and say goodnight
I won't go to sleep without monsters for the night
These flapping fairies give me a fright
They're tiny creatures with glittery wings
Smelling like candyfloss, those annoying little things
I miss my monsters and their naughty ways
Sneaking out of my house and into the caves
I hope morning comes soon, ready for a brand new day
I hope my monsters are on their way.

Ruben McQuillan (9)
St Teresa's Catholic Primary School, Ashford

The Famous Footballer

I stand on the field with my heart beating fast
Waiting for my teammate to pass
So I make my run into the space
I beat the last defender with my amazing brain

I take my first touch and have the ball at my feet
Should I pass or should I shoot?
There's only the keeper to beat
So Messi and Ronaldo have been here before
It's my time to shine and make the parents roar
Goal!
That was Jesse Saffa.

Aldy Saffa (9)
St Teresa's Catholic Primary School, Ashford

Dogs

C lever like clockwork, their heads are always ticking
O mnivores, they eat almost anything
M any breeds, variety is the spice of life
P erfect in every way
A migo, always there for you
N aughty, only sometimes
I ntelligent, you'll be surprised what they can learn!
O h! Another mess on the floor
N oisy, always barking.

Emilia Rebecca Skinner (9)
St Teresa's Catholic Primary School, Ashford

Unicorns

U nder the rainbow I found a unicorn
N o one has ever seen a unicorn but me
I believe in the unicorn I saw
C ould there be more?
O range flames came out of its nostrils
R ed beautiful hair was flowing through it's mane
N ever ever had I thought I would see such a stunning horn
S urely I will see it again soon.

Gabriella Charlotte Pigram (9)
St Teresa's Catholic Primary School, Ashford

Summer

Summertime, my favourite time of the year
What a beautiful day
I wake up with a smile on my face
Fun on the beach and fun in the park
Riding my bike and playing with my friends
What a beautiful day
Dancing, singing and playing games
Swimming in water to cool me down
Nothing is stopping me from having fun
What a beautiful day.

Isabel Johny (9)
St Teresa's Catholic Primary School, Ashford

Footballer

There I stood ready to play
With my teammates we could say,
"Today will be our day!"

At Repton Manor playground
I played, tackled and ran around
I scored and heard the cheering sound

It was a warm day in summer
We won because we played better
My dream is to be a footballer.

Munashe Parsvell Mungoni (9)
St Teresa's Catholic Primary School, Ashford

Avengers

A vengers ready I see
V ery tall like Hulk can be
E nemies coming, it's time to fight
N ow get them before day turns to night
G o back to the base
E very weapon in a secret place
R eady for another day
S ay goodnight then go away.

Riley McQuillan (9)
St Teresa's Catholic Primary School, Ashford

Summer

S un blazing through the tall trees
U mbrellas shading people from the blazing sun
M aking sandcastles on the beach
M ucking around in the paddling pool
E ating delicious food from the sizzling barbecue
R unning around in the boiling hot sun having fun.

Jessica Broome (9)
St Teresa's Catholic Primary School, Ashford

Small Jungle Dream

I opened my door to see what was outside
It was a small jungle
Where the river ran and the animals were free

I saw a tiger walk past, it scared me a bit, but it roared hello
A little monkey climbed on my back and said, "Stay forever, please don't go."
The big rhino was in the pool whilst zebras ran past us and left little marks in the sand
Koalas munched on bamboo sticks in front of me

Swinging from vine to vine was so much fun
Then my mum came and ruined the fun, saying, "Sweetie, time for school."
Hopefully I'll dream more tonight
"Sleep tight little jungle."

Ruby Rae Mandry-Lowe (10)
Sundridge & Brasted CE (VC) Primary School, Sundridge

Follow Your Dreams

F ollow your dreams
O nly my horse that matters
L ive your life where you're free
L ove everyone who cares about you
O pen your life to new beginnings
W ait for the right moment

Y ou must hold on to your dreams
O ur dreams are important to me and my horse
U nbearable dreams
R ide it

D on't let fear get in your way
R emember all of it
E njoy it whilst it lasts
A im for the top
M e here with my horse
S tart your own dream.

Daisy Morgan (11)
Sundridge & Brasted CE (VC) Primary School, Sundridge

Dreams And Nightmares

These creatures are nocturnal
They each have different emotions
Some leap, some help, some fly in the sky
Their habitats live in a young, imaginative mind
Nightmares roar while dreams soar
In dreams you wear a crown
Nightmares take over with clowns
Dreams splash the crystal-like water
Nightmares thrash and turn their prey to mush
Sun whites, while moon fights
Unicorns are neat, wolves create weeps
The sun is creeping up, we need to say bye to our friends
Till the dark of night, when we will meet again.

Zachary Alex Harvey (11)
Sundridge & Brasted CE (VC) Primary School, Sundridge

To The Moon I Go!

I wake up to see a beautiful bike
Could it be?
I decide to ride it willingly
The wind blows me up, up and away
To the shiny moon where I will stay
But when I get there I see no one waiting for me
Suddenly, I see a glow, just a spider as you shall know
How it could have got here, I don't know
But who cares? I'm on top of the top of the Earth itself!
Spider bites and runs away, I turn into an alien, hooray!
This is my dream.

Tayla Rendle (10)
Sundridge & Brasted CE (VC) Primary School, Sundridge

Nightmares

N ightmares do not exist, I tell myself
I cannot bear it anymore
G o away I tell them, the clowns laugh more
H orror they implore
T remble, I tremble, scared all over
M irrors, I run to go to the bathroom, I see them in the mirrors
A bad dream, that's what it is
R eally scary, that is what they are
E nd is what they do
S top is what I say.

Chelsea Casserley (10)
Sundridge & Brasted CE (VC) Primary School, Sundridge

Dreams

Dreams are mysterious things
You could fly and grow wings
No one knows where they come from
Or whether they last that long

Dreams come from nowhere
They could have a poisonous pear
Unicorns fly high
But no one knows why

Dreams make you think
Like a princess will wink
You don't know where to go
So follow the flow

Dreams, dreams, dreams.

Oscar Samways (11)
Sundridge & Brasted CE (VC) Primary School, Sundridge

Love And Hate

L eaving all my friends behind
O ver and over, I'd watched others die
V ery nervous, but ready
E veryone was counting on me

A s soon as it began
N obody saw it coming
D evilish hate enabled transformation

H appy as could be
A n explosion was made
T o my surprise
E veryone survived.

Jared Douglas Somerville (11)
Sundridge & Brasted CE (VC) Primary School, Sundridge

The Ocean Universe

One day in a universe like an ocean
Bobbing up and down like a jack-in-a-box
A mile in the future seeing turtles playing volleyball
Underneath the water coral like rainbows
Catfish buying Lamborghinis
Turtles flying with wings down below with dolphins
Gliding bluebirds searching, it's time to go.

Oscar Shadforth (10)
Sundridge & Brasted CE (VC) Primary School, Sundridge

Heaven Can Be Weird

Heaven can be weird because
As I become awake I realise I'm in a completely white land
I am confused, three unicorns come along and say hi
I am about to say bye
When they tell me their names
And they turn out to be my friends!
Heaven can be weird sometimes.

Harri Stubbings (11)
Sundridge & Brasted CE (VC) Primary School, Sundridge

Midnight Dreams

Midnight dreams
Midnight dreams
Come join me in my world
Of a fantasy theme
Midnight dreams, fairy dust, sparkle
My friends they are
Riley my unicorn, my best friend so far

As I swish through the clouds
And sway through the stars
I see a magical world beneath me
Full of candy bars!

I jump on my unicorn
And the fairies come out
As I fly through the chocolate galaxy
And Mars and Milky Way stars!

As I float to the ground
I hear boiling and bubbling
Like there's a cauldron
Somewhere around
Out of nowhere
There comes a mysterious man
With short grubby magical hands

Reaching out to send me home
I wake up in my bed alone.

Alana Heywood-Oriogun (9)
The Gateway Primary Academy, Dartford

Mythical Dreams

One fairy here
One fairy there
There are fairies everywhere!

What is that I see
Peering through the leaves of a tree?
A pearl-white horn and a shake of a tail
A galaxy mare so gentle and frail
And a joyful voice says,
"What are you doing here?"
I quietly reply,
"I'm here to adventure, I have no fear."
A pearl-white unicorn
Suddenly I see
She has holographic hooves and a white horn
She says, "Climb on my back."
Then we fly through the sky, so dark and black
But as I reach to touch the sweet fur on her head
I wake up in my warm bed.

Clara Madalina Petcu (9)
The Gateway Primary Academy, Dartford

Underwater Dream

As my turquoise tail splashed into the shimmering ocean,
I dreamt I was a beautiful metallic mermaid swimming into the depths of the deep blue sea,
Out of the corner of my eye, I spotted a pearlescent oyster sitting in the pure golden sand,
As I glided like a dolphin towards the wonderful sight,
I was amazed by an enormous blue whale swimming by,
What a beautiful mammal it was,
As I headed towards the oyster, the shell began to open up, out shone a bright white light,
I wondered what it was...
By the time I approached the oyster, it was fully open,
And inside I could see a faraway galaxy sky.

Lily Barden (8)
The Gateway Primary Academy, Dartford

The Sweet Unicorn World

What's here I wonder
I hear hooves trotting along around me
It is Galaxy the unicorn
She has a luscious galaxy mane and tail
Her pink eyes shimmer in the twilight
Like shooting stars in the faraway sky
Her graceful body leaps
She holds a metallic and holographic rainbow horn
Upon her pearlescent white fur
As fast as a flash
She flies in the wind, taking me into the world
Faraway in space
As I approach the world, it's filled with joy
And happiness throughout the land.

Emilia Nathanael (8)
The Gateway Primary Academy, Dartford

Nightmares

N ightmares are terrifying
I try to leave but darkness holds me back
G hosts and monsters kill my dreams
H aunting my head, making me dizzy
T error goes into my head, into my heart
M aking me shake, I watch in horror
A lso nightmares make me tremble
R eality and dreams fuse together
E very time sleep is said, it sends shivers down my spine
S leepless nights filled with nightmares.

Neve McDonald Murray (8)
The Gateway Primary Academy, Dartford

A Fairy Dream

I am going to sleep
Now what do I see?
I open my eyes, I see fairies
Dancing around me

I ask the fairies, "How do you fly?"
Now they carry me high in the sky
I am in the clouds, what shall I do?
I'll flap my magic wings like a butterfly
I am landing, I see everyone cheer

I touch a fairy, it's ever so near
Now I see I am in my warm bed
Magical dreams filling my head.

Sruthi Edara (8)
The Gateway Primary Academy, Dartford

Nightmare

N ightmares are bad, so very bad
I hate them so much
G hosts and monsters making me sad
H ound my dreams and such
T errible, terrible things, I can't talk
M aking my dreams evil and scary
A lone in my room, too afraid to walk
R ustling noises under my bed, making me wary
E very dark corner makes me feel creepy.

Isla McDonald Murray (8)
The Gateway Primary Academy, Dartford

Gummyland

Gummyland, oh lovely Gummyland
You come to me at night
A gummy tree, a gummy train
And oddly, a gummy light
Gummyland, oh dreamy Gummyland
I swim in a gummy pool
Also I jump on a gummy trampoline
Ew! Look at that gummy ogre drool
Gummyland, oh crazy Gummyland
Gumminess everywhere
Gummy, gummy gummies are delicious
Gummies, even my gummy teddy bear!

Benjamin Leachman (9)
The Gateway Primary Academy, Dartford

The Dark Fairy

I go to bed but the dark fairy haunts my dream
But luckily I have my magic team
But every night it's the same
The dark fairy comes to play
Now that everyone has gone away
I cannot sleep, not even today
Scratch, scratch behind my bed
Second day, I see her head...
The haunting spirit is in the gloom.

Daniela Guwor (8)
The Gateway Primary Academy, Dartford

Candy

I open my eyes, what do I see?
What is in front of me?
I look to the left, I look to the right
Then I take a big bite
It tastes so sweet like a strawberry
Melting in my hand
Now I'm in Candyland
Now I know what is in front of me
Lots and lots of sweet candy
My dream becomes a reality!

Andrew Gray (7)
The Gateway Primary Academy, Dartford

Flying Unicorn

I close my eyes...
Suddenly I find myself in the stormy sky
Flying high and high from the silver fluffy clouds below
Her soft hair tickling my head
I trust and know that she won't drop me ahead
My unicorn flies away to another lovely dream
I'll see you in my next dream.

Eva Odetah (7)
The Gateway Primary Academy, Dartford

Unicorns

U nicorns are fluffy and fair
N eat, furry mane and hair
I wish we could one day meet
C uddly, soft and sweet
O h I have never had a dream like this
R emember what I see in this
N early don't want to get up from this dream.

Scarlett Eve Leachman (7)
The Gateway Primary Academy, Dartford

Fairy Dreams

Little fairies having fun
With some giggles, sparkles and fun
Rainbows and sunshine everywhere
Gleaming down on toadstools with lovely care
This surely is the sweetest dream
Full of happiness and love it would seem.

Jessica Hawney (8)
The Gateway Primary Academy, Dartford

Candy

C andy is colourful and beautiful
A nd as sweet as can be
N anny's sweet treats are the best
D reams are made of jars of sweets
Y ummy, yum, yum for me!

Lacey Underhill (7)
The Gateway Primary Academy, Dartford

YoungWriters
Est.1991

YOUNG WRITERS INFORMATION

We hope you have enjoyed reading this book – and that you will continue to in the coming years.

If you're a young writer who enjoys reading and creative writing, or the parent of an enthusiastic poet or story writer, do visit our website **www.youngwriters.co.uk**. Here you will find free competitions, workshops and games, as well as recommended reads, a poetry glossary and our blog.

If you would like to order further copies of this book, or any of our other titles, then please give us a call or visit **www.youngwriters.co.uk**.

Young Writers
Remus House
Coltsfoot Drive
Peterborough
PE2 9BF
(01733) 890066
info@youngwriters.co.uk